Seasons

by Peggy Gavan
illustrated by Susan T. Hall

Troll Associates

Something to Think About...

Did you know that it takes the earth 365 days
to make a complete trip around the sun?
That's one whole year!

What things happen in winter?

What things happen in summer?

What do farmers do in the spring?

What do animals do during the different seasons?

LIBRARY OF CONGRESS CATALOGING-IN-PUBLICATION DATA

Gavan, Peggy.
  Seasons / by Peggy Gavan; illustrated by Susan T. Hall.
     p.   cm.— (First-start science)
  ISBN 0-8167-3605-7 (lib.)   ISBN 0-8167-3606-5 (pbk.)
  1. Seasons—Juvenile literature.   [1. Seasons.]   I. Hall, Susan
T., ill.   II. Title.   III. Series
  QB637.4.G38   1994
  525'.5—dc20   94-26981

Printed in the United States of America.

10 9 8 7 6 5 4 3 2

Winter, spring, summer, autumn.
These are the four seasons of the year.

Why do the seasons change?

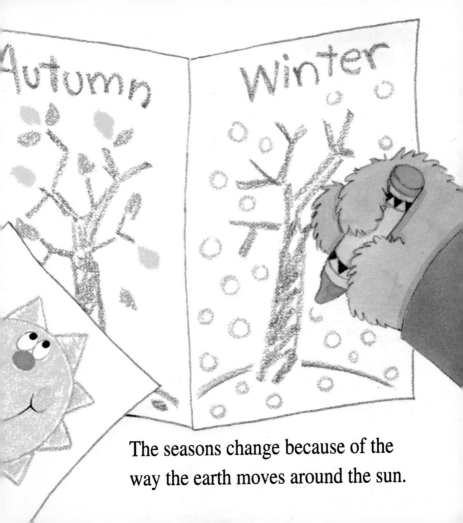

The seasons change because of the way the earth moves around the sun.

The Big Trip

The amount of sunshine changes as the earth travels around the sun. It takes one year for the earth to make one trip around the sun.

The Small Turn

The earth also spins like a top. When part of the earth turns toward the sun, it is day. When that part turns away from the sun, it is night. It takes 24 hours for the earth to make one complete turn.

As the earth spins around the sun,
it also leans,
or tilts.

Summer

One part of the earth tilts away from the sun for part of the year. Then it tilts toward the sun for part of the year.

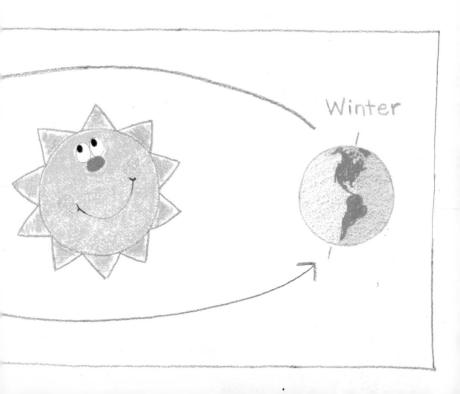

Winter

When it is winter where you live, your part
of the earth is tilted away from the sun.
Your part of the earth gets less sunshine,
so the air is colder.

In winter, the days are short and the nights are long.

Animals find warm places to sleep.

Then your part of the earth begins to slowly tilt
toward the sun.
The air gets warmer. The days get longer.

Spring is here!

In the spring, the snow melts away.
Farmers plant seeds in the soil.

Baby animals play in the green grass.

Then your part of the earth tilts even closer to the sun. The days are longer and hotter.

It is summer!

In the summer, plants grow bigger and bigger.

Baby animals grow bigger, too!

Next, your part of the earth begins to tilt away from the sun. The days are shorter. The air is cooler

It is autumn!

In autumn, some leaves change color.

The animals get busy storing their food.
They know that winter is coming again!

Around and around the earth spins.
Around and around the sun it goes.

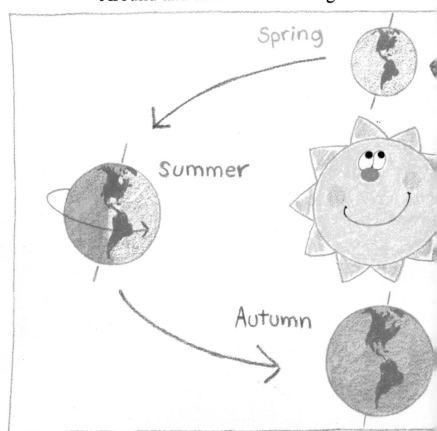

Your part of the earth tilts toward the sun.
It tilts away from the sun.

Winter, spring, summer, autumn.
Which season is your favorite?